Self-Realization

FOUNDED IN 1925 BY PARAMAHANSA YOGANANDA

**A Magazine Devoted to
Healing of Body, Mind, and Soul**

Healing the body of disease by proper diet, right living, and recharging the body with God's all-powerful cosmic energy; removing inharmonies and inefficiency from the mind by concentration, constructive thinking, and cheerfulness; and freeing the ever perfect soul from the bonds of spiritual ignorance by meditation.

FALL 2018	VOL. 89, NO. 4	ISSN 0037-1564

Front Cover: Golden Lotus Archway at Self-Realization Fellowship Lake Shrine, Pacific Palisades, California

Opposite: Paramahansa Yogananda, 1949

"When human will refuses to acknowledge its limitations, then it becomes divine will."

Featured CD recording for this issue:

BECOMING HUMBLE BEARERS OF LIGHT

In this talk presented at the 2009 SRF World Convocation, Brother Ishtananda elucidates with wit and wisdom how to turn away from negativity and cultivate a positive outlook on life, thereby influencing others for the good.

"If you need to calm down, you really should take a deep breath. It's just what the neuroscientists ordered."

SELF-REALIZATION (ISSN 0037-1564) Vol. 89, No. 4 issued Fall 2018, is published quarterly by Self-Realization Fellowship, 3880 San Rafael Avenue, Los Angeles, California 90065. Founder, Paramahansa Yogananda. President, Brother Chidananda. Subscriptions — U.S. and possessions: $19.00 yearly; three years, $54.00. International airmail $23.00 yearly; three years, $66.00. One issue, $6.00. Periodicals postage paid at Los Angeles, California. POSTMASTER: Send address changes to SELF-REALIZATION, 3880 San Rafael Avenue, Los Angeles, California 90065-3219. Printed on recycled paper ♲ Copyright © 2018 Self-Realization Fellowship. All rights reserved. No part of *Self-Realization* magazine — text, photographs, or other material — may be reproduced in any form or transmitted by any means (electronic, mechanical, or otherwise) including photocopy, recording, or any information storage and retrieval system, without written permission from Self-Realization Fellowship.

Yoga

The Quintessence of Spirituality

A talk by
Brother Chidananda
President of SRF/YSS

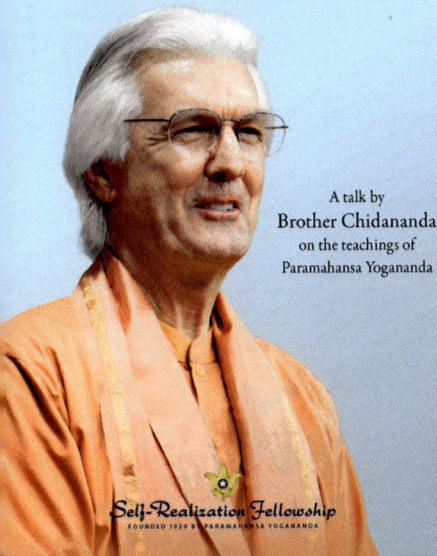

Yoga

THE QUINTESSENCE OF SPIRITUALITY

A talk by
Brother Chidananda
on the teachings of
Paramahansa Yogananda

Self-Realization Fellowship
FOUNDED 1920 BY PARAMAHANSA YOGANANDA

DVD $19.95

This inspired talk was delivered at the 2017 YSS Sharad Sangam in Ranchi, India, as part of the YSS Centenary celebrations. In it, Brother Chidananda elucidates three core concepts of yoga — *sadhana, satsanga,* and *darshan* — in light of Paramahansa Yogananda's teachings, bringing out the most elevated and practical meaning of these ancient terms.

Topics Include:

- The essence of India's eternal Truth, encapsulated in the science of Yoga that Paramahansa Yogananda brought to the world
- Utilizing the integrated system of SRF meditation techniques in the search for the Divine
- Practical ways of making the Divine Presence a reality in one's life
- The inner experience of attuning oneself to the presence of the guru
- A special guided meditation at the close of the talk

AWAKENING
for Success an

By Paramahansa Yogananda

*A talk given on January 25, 1935.**

The purpose of human life consists in finding out what we really are. We can inquire what human life is because we are endowed with the faculty of reason. The distinctive difference between man and animal is that man has the ability to reason and inquire into the source and meaning of his existence, and of the existence of other forms of life. Yet many human beings behave more blindly than animals, going sheeplike to the slaughterhouse of death without ever having sought the answer to the mystery of life.

Original painting of
Paramahansa Yogananda
by K. Dezso-Shealy

---

* Much of this talk was integrated into the *Self-Realization Fellowship Lessons* in the 1930s. In preparing it for publication in a forthcoming volume of Paramahansaji's *Collected Talks and Essays,* unused material from the original talk, never before published, has been added.

WILL POWER

Divine Accomplishment

Whence did reason come? What is its source? It is intuition, the omniscient faculty of the soul, that fathers the faculties of reason and discrimination. We must daily recharge our reason and good judgment by contact with the soul through deep meditation if we are to achieve true success and fulfill the purpose of our earthly sojourn.

DIFFERENCE BETWEEN "WISH" AND "WILL"

To wish and to will are different things. In this life we see that people are following many different paths to one common goal: all are seeking happiness. Some want money, some want health, others want fame, hoping that through these they will find happiness. Varied are the desires, but few persons have the will power to accomplish them.

And how desires come and go in the mind! Do you realize how many of them have found a place in your heart? Within every human being lies a great graveyard of unfulfilled desires. Desires that you feel cannot be fulfilled corrode the heart, and are really just "wishes." Sometimes you hear someone say, "I wish I were a king," or something equally unlikely. These are wishes that you know cannot be fulfilled. And not all people have the same desires. In the zoological garden of life roam all kinds of animals of desires; what interests one person doesn't necessarily have any attraction for someone else.

But remember this: To have a desire fulfilled, you must first have the power to fulfill it. A wish is a desire that you think cannot come true. Stronger than "wish" is "intention" — intention to do a thing or to satisfy some wish or desire. But

> *"When human will refuses to acknowledge its limitations, then it becomes divine will. Whenever you meet resistance, do not give up."*

"will" consists of desire plus energy — a motivating desire plus application of energy to bring that desire to fruition. Will means continuous, concentrated action until that desire is fulfilled.

How few persons actually will! Of course one should not use will power to perform wrong actions: that is a violation of the purpose of will within us, and brings us harm. Will should be guided by wisdom. Right desires, and will guided by wisdom, lead to ultimate fulfillment in God.

There is a difference between ineffectual desires and the kind of persistent longing that eventually materializes its object in reality. Desire involves a strong psychological wish; but longing connotes an unbearable, haunting desire that unfailingly gathers to itself the necessary force and knowledge with which to materialize itself. Therefore, dear friends, remember that you will not achieve merely by a series of wishes or desires. You will succeed by nurturing your worthy, wholesome desire into a heartfelt, undying longing; and then manifesting that longing in continuous, introspective, intelligent activity.

WHY DO PEOPLE FAIL IN LIFE?

Do you know why people fail? It is because they give up. I often say that if I had no job, I would shake up the whole world so that it would be glad to give me a job to keep me quiet. *You must exercise your will power.* If you make up your mind and go forth like a flame, every obstacle in your path will be consumed. The man of realization walks safely even where bullets fly, for the divine will is behind him.

Let me tell you a story: A and B were fighting. After a long time A — exhausted — said to himself: "I cannot continue any longer." But B thought: "Just one more punch, though I can hardly move." He gave it, and down went A.

If you think that you cannot go on any longer and then you make an extra effort, you will see that divine will begins to reinforce your will. When human will refuses to acknowledge its limitations, then it becomes divine will. Whenever you meet resistance, do not give up. If you go on exercising your will power, you will suddenly find that your will has become linked with divine will.

Rouse this will power from the sleep of ignorance. How can you develop it? Choose some objective that you think you cannot accomplish, and then try with all your might to do that one thing. When you have achieved success, go on to something bigger and keep on exercising your will power in this way. If your difficulty is great, deeply pray: "Lord, give me the power to conquer all my difficulties." You must *use* your will power, no matter what you are, or who you are. *You must make up your mind*. Use this will power both in business and in meditation. There is no greater enemy of your own happiness than yourself when you slouch through life with a paralytic will and an indifferent attitude.

"Persons of active will, like the sparkling diamond, make themselves receptive to the sunlight of God's omnipresent power...."

Remember, the power of God's will is in all of you. But some persons are like diamonds and others are like coal. Persons of active will, like the sparkling diamond, make themselves receptive to the sunlight of God's omnipresent power of accomplishment and allow it to flow through them. Ordinary individuals of passive mentality make themselves like the dull piece of coal; the sunlight of God's all-accomplishing will, though shining on them, does not illumine their lives with brilliant achievements. Never let laziness or passivity obstruct your noble material and spiritual goals.

By Will Power, Charge Your Success Thoughts With Dynamic Force

Such will power lies within you that if you really put it to use there is nothing you could not accomplish. Will power has created everything — even your body. It is the will that leads you from one desire to another until with all your might you try to succeed in accomplishing your greatest desires. Rarely do people develop the true potentiality of will power! The will develops in man by normal evolutionary progress, but its evolution may be hastened by right thinking and acting.

Carrying a thought with dynamic will power means holding to it until that thought pattern develops dynamic force. When a thought is made dynamic by will force, it can create or rearrange the atoms into the desired pattern according to the mental blueprint you have created. When you continuously develop your will until its dynamic force manifests, you can heal others by your will power; you can say, as Jesus said to the leper, "I will; be thou clean."* You can control your destiny by will power; you can command a mountain, "Be thou removed, and be thou cast into the sea; it shall be done."†

How to Develop Your Will and Guide It by Wisdom

Many people think they should not use their own will power to accomplish what they desire, lest they interfere in some way with God's plan or the scheme of life. They passively accept that "this is how life is meant to be." It is a great mistake to believe you should not use your will; and in any case, that is impossible. In order not to use will power you would have to lie down and not move at all. If you move even a finger, you are using your will power. You must use will power even to eat.

---

* Matthew 8:3.
† Matthew 21:21.

The only time your will power is inactive is when you are under chloroform or are otherwise rendered unconscious. When the power to will leaves the body entirely, one dies.

It is true that human will guided by ignorance is bad; it leads to error and unhappiness. But when human will is guided by wisdom to right actions, and thus tuned in with divine will, it then operates for our highest welfare and happiness. That is what Jesus meant when he said: "Thy will be done." God wishes us to tune in with divine will, that we may be guided by His wisdom to find the real fulfillment of all our desires, in Him.

"When human will is guided by wisdom to right actions, and thus tuned in with divine will, it then operates for our highest welfare and happiness."

Some people think that just by virtue of prayer God will listen to them and fulfill their desires. But this is laziness. It is necessary to exercise will power, to strive to tune it with the divine will. When your will revolves continually around one definite purpose, it becomes *dynamic* will. This is the quality of will power possessed by Jesus and by all other great sons of God.

The power behind your will is the will of God. This is the way to develop your will:

1. Before you will to do a thing, reason as to what you should do.
2. Make sure that you are directing your will toward accomplishing something good and helpful to yourself.
3. Pray to God to reinforce your will with His divine will.
4. Exert your will through right action until you achieve your goal.

Don't be passive. Your will was given to you so that you may use it and become a conqueror. Remember, in your will is the will of God. It is His power that you use.

Your Development of Will Power Carries Over to Future Incarnations

According to the law of karma that governs all human actions, persons who have developed strong will find themselves the possessor of the same adamant will in their next incarnation. According to the law of cause and effect, the effect is equal to the cause. Thus it is good to develop will even to the last stage of life, for then it becomes a very powerful ally of accomplishment in the next life.

Therefore, my friends, see to it that each day you select one wholesome desire and use your will and reason throughout that day until you accomplish your goal.

Technique of Increasing Your Will Power Day by Day

In the morning, before you start working, select a particular longing that will improve your or your family's material, moral, or spiritual well-being; and try to accomplish it with bulldog tenacity and clever planning. Write it down and keep it with you throughout the day. If you can't accomplish it, owing to faulty methods or wrong environment, then seek expert advice. Compare your method and plan of action for that specific achievement with that of others who have demonstrated or proved better plans for action. Change your environment if necessary in order to accomplish your purpose. You, being the proud possessor of dynamic will, must never give up until "by hook or crook," as they say, you are able to obtain the desired results. In this way, as you achieve the completion of even a small but definite goal each day, you will gain more and more confidence in the power of your will and thus increase its accomplishing strength.

You will find most people fail to achieve the necessary

Paramahansa Yogananda

The Divine Romance

THE DIVINE ROMANCE

COLLECTED TALKS AND ESSAYS ON
REALIZING GOD IN DAILY LIFE,
VOLUME II

by
Paramahansa Yogananda

PARAMAHANSA YOGANANDA
(January 5, 1893–March 7, 1952)

2   3

eBOOKS

More than two dozen ebook titles are now available

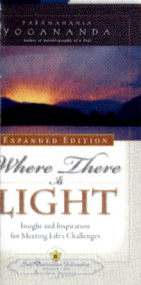
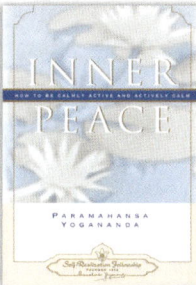
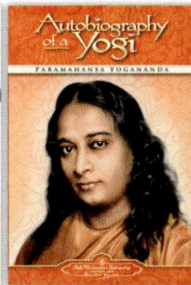
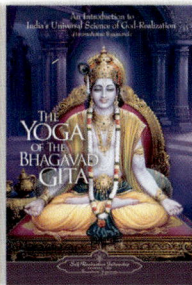
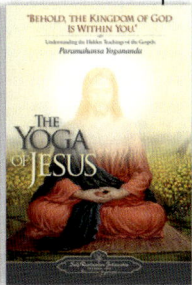

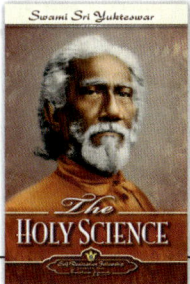
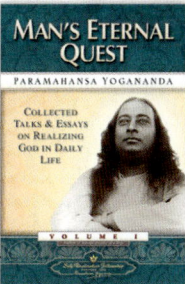
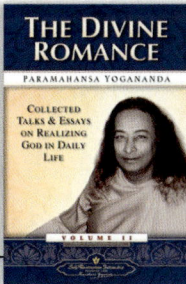
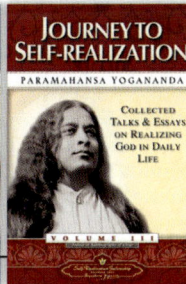

> *"While thousands remain dreaming by the wayside, or become despondent and give up after a few unsuccessful tries at success, the individual of dynamic will continually moves along the path of success until the goal is reached."*

necessities of material life, mental happiness, or God-realization because they don't employ the above-mentioned technique of developing will by accomplishing something noble and difficult every day. While thousands remain dreaming by the wayside, or become despondent and give up after a few unsuccessful tries at success, the individual of dynamic will continually moves along the path of success until the goal is reached. I have exercised this will and have accomplished much in this life. That will power shall come if you learn and practice the great truths of Yogoda, the Self-Realization Fellowship techniques.*

THE VALUE OF "WON'T" POWER

There is another factor in developing wisdom-guided will power. The saints say: "Do not be a slave to your senses. Let nothing control you. Your senses are given to serve you, not to be your tyrannical ruler." As soon as your discrimination points out that any sense enjoyment has become detrimental to your health or happiness, remember: that is a "sin" you must overcome by virtue. Virtue means that which bestows lasting happiness and well-being of body, mind, and soul.

In your efforts to govern your life by self-control, try to develop your "won't" power if you haven't yet enough will power. For instance, when you are at the dinner table and Mr. Greed lures you to eat more than you should, and tries to chloroform your self-control and cast you into the pit of indigestion, watch yourself. After partaking of the right quality and quantity of food, just say to yourself with firm resolve: "I won't eat any

---

* Taught in the *Self-Realization Fellowship Lessons.*

more," and get up from your chair at the table and deliberately walk away. It often seems difficult to exercise will power, but it is easy to develop won't power. Discrimination, not habit, should be the constant guide of our conduct; and the best antidote for bad habits is won't power.

THE HIGHEST USE OF WILL POWER IS TO FIND GOD

In your heart you must love nothing more than God, who is a "jealous" God. If you want God, you must have the will to cast away from your heart every desire but the desire for Him. And if you really want God, nothing can touch you to deter you from that desire. Have only one desire: "May Thy love shine forever on the sanctuary of my devotion, and may I be able to awaken Thy love in all hearts." That is my only prayer. I don't even pray for my body. I don't want to enjoy God alone; I want to establish the consciousness of God in the hearts of all. So always remember that the greatest and highest use of will is to will for God alone. God is imperishable and with God everything good will come. Develop your will power. Turn your will power away from worldly desires; it is wasted on them. Look at this life as nothing but a dream. Make up your mind to will for God.

"We can make even our greatest difficulties and failures our steppingstones on the upward climb toward success."

If you know that you have got to find God in order to satisfy soul-hunger within; and if you use your will power, then you will find Him. But God will not answer unless you know the law. Again and again you must fire the shells of your prayer and will power to break down the ramparts of God's silence. He is castled in silence, but if you send shell after shell of concentration and meditation, the walls will break and God's glory will burst forth.

When Lord Buddha sought illumination, he sat under a banyan tree and said:

Beneath the banyan bough
On sacred seat I take this vow:
"Until life's mystery I solve,
Until I gain the Priceless Lore,
Though bones and fleeting flesh dissolve,
I'll leave this posture nevermore."

Buddha succeeded in his divine quest. Such a will becomes one with the Divine Will.

Two Frogs in Trouble
A story by Paramahansa Yogananda

Once a big fat frog and a lively little frog were hopping along together when they had the misfortune to jump straight into a pail of fresh milk. They swam for hours and hours, hoping to get out somehow; but the sides of the pail were steep and slippery, and death seemed certain.

When the big frog was exhausted he lost courage. There seemed no hope of rescue. "Why keep struggling against the inevitable? I can't swim any longer," he moaned. "Keep on! Keep on!" urged the little frog, who was still circling the pail. So they went on for a while. But the big frog decided it was no use. "Little brother, we may as well give up," he gasped, "I'm going to quit struggling."

Now only the little frog was left. He thought to himself, "Well, to give up is to be dead, so I will keep on swimming. Two more hours passed and the tiny legs of the determined little frog were almost paralyzed with exhaustion. It seemed as if he could not keep moving for another minute. But then he thought of his dead friend, and repeated, "To give up is to be meat for someone's table, so I'll keep on paddling until I die — if death is to come — but I will not cease trying — 'while there is life, there's hope!'"

That is the kind of will and determination that shall give you salvation. Give these teachings your undivided attention, and continuously cooperate with what I am urging you. Sincere souls who are really seeking God shall find Him who alone can satisfy the unslaked thirst and longings of our hearts. Many thousands have listened to my talks, but few have truly put into action what they have heard. Those who do shall find the mighty Truth — the Love and Glory Divine which is everywhere — manifesting through their consciousness evermore. ❏

Intoxicated with determination, the little frog kept on, around and around and around the pail, chopping the milk into white waves. After a while, just as he felt completely numb and thought he was about to drown, he suddenly felt something solid under him. To his astonishment, he saw that he was resting on a lump of butter which he had churned by his incessant paddling! And so the successful little frog leaped out of the milk pail to freedom.

Remember, to persevere and never give up is to develop will power and the ability to win in everything we undertake. We are all in the slippery milk pail of life, like the two frogs, trying to get out of our troubles and inharmonies. Most people give up and therefore fail, like the big frog. In order to succeed, we must be like the determined little frog who persevered. Then we will churn an opportunity by our God-guided, unflinching will, and be able to hop out of the milk pail of limitations and difficulties and move onward to freedom and eternal success.

A life without trouble and vicissitudes is a life without progress. We can make even our greatest difficulties and failures our steppingstones on the upward climb toward success.

A Willing Captive of God's Love

By Sri Daya Mata

President of SRF/YSS from 1955 until her passing in 2010

From a satsanga with ashram residents at Self-Realization Fellowship Mother Center, Los Angeles, California, December 1960

> I fled Him, down the nights and down the days;
> I fled Him, down the arches of the years;...
>
> I said to Dawn: Be sudden — to Eve: Be soon;
> With thy young skiey blossoms heap me over
> From this tremendous Lover....
>
> — Francis Thompson, "The Hound of Heaven"

We have spent incarnations fleeing from that Divine One, the "Hound of Heaven." But finally the devotee ceases his flight and becomes a willing captive of the Divine Beloved. Such thrills of love! No words can fully describe the joy, the ecstasy, the love one feels when the soul's longing and hunger for God are satisfied.

Francis Thompson describes God as the Divine Lover. And so He is. Before Him, we are all feminine; the Divine is the only positive or male principle. Ultimately every saint realizes this.* Before Him, we are souls. We must similarly free our consciousness from identification with this fleshly form that decays and grows ugly, and that constantly tries to drag the mind down to a lower level. Don't give in to the dictates of the body. The soul must be the ruler of your life.

The soul is immortal, ever pure, capable of expressing the highest love and receiving the highest joy. Don't settle for less in this world. Nothing else is worth it, for in the end each one finds, as the poet goes on to say, "All things betray thee, who betrayest Me....Naught shelters thee, who wilt not shelter Me." Everything in life eventually betrays or disillusions the soul, leaving a great emptiness within. Try as we may to fill that void with human friendship and companionship, with worldly pursuits and possessions, nothing can fill that vacuum but the Divine Beloved. We cannot be permanently satisfied with anything less than God. So meditate deeply. Cry in the wilderness of your heart for the one Love: "Night and day, night and day, I look for Thee night and day."† That must be the constant yearning of the devotee. May even one among you hearken to those beautiful words of Gurudeva Paramahansa Yogananda.

Master said: "One moon gives more light than all the stars." The mooned life of one true devotee sheds more light of God's

---

* St. John of the Cross, for example, often referred to the soul as the bride of God or of Christ.

† From "Door of My Heart" in *Cosmic Chants,* by Paramahansa Yogananda.

goodness and love than all the twinkling lives that glimmer only with human love. With the devotion of a heart filled with longing for the one Beloved, sing unceasingly to God alone: "Night and day I am looking for You, my Lord, night and day."

DEEP MEDITATION FANS DIVINE DESIRE

To find God you have to be adamant, willing to brush aside every deterrent, ruthlessly if necessary. You have to be a divine warrior, like Arjuna,* facing and battling every obstacle, determined to let nothing stand between you and the object of your desire, God. Thus is the Lord found. He who is lukewarm in devotion and weak in his pursuit will never come to know what tremendous love and joy God is. Meditate deeply, every day — if only for five minutes — making every moment count. For that period, however brief, lose sight of the world; call to God in the great hall of silence within. Cry to Him with all the yearning of your soul; that's the way we learned to meditate with Guruji.

You have to keep fanning the little ember of divine desire with devotion and meditation until that spark becomes an all-consuming flame. That blaze burns out all dross — human weakness and gross desires — in one all-consuming, purifying fire of divine desire, love, wisdom, joy. Love, wisdom, joy: that is what God is. And that is what contact with God gives. Don't be satisfied until you have Him.

We must know God even as Christ, Krishna, Buddha, and all the great ones experienced Him. The Lord loves each one of us with the same intensity that He loved them. But on our part we have not been willing to put forth the necessary effort to receive that love. We allow ourselves to be consumed with the little passing pleasures of this world, and with hurt feelings, moods, and frustrated desires. Who among you has but one desire, for God alone — caring for naught else? Lay your lesser desires at the feet of God. When you have found Him,

---

* The devotee-hero of the Bhagavad Gita.

He will satisfy all other desires. Your part is to strive eagerly toward fulfillment of the one supreme longing, to experience God's presence within and without.

"You have to keep fanning the little ember of divine desire with devotion and meditation until that spark becomes an all-consuming flame."

TRY ALWAYS TO GIVE LOVE TO ALL

The Bible teaches us: "Love the Lord thy God with all thy heart," meaning with all your love; "with all thy mind," meaning with a mind that doesn't wander but is fixed on God; "and with all thy soul."* You are the soul; and as you realize this and learn to love God purely, unconditionally, then, in the reunion of your soul with Him, you will understand what it means to "love thy neighbor as thyself."† The scripture doesn't say "love thy friends and thy loved ones," but "love thy neighbor." Thy neighbor is whomsoever God puts in your path, your friend and your enemy. "Love thy neighbor as thyself" means to love all.

At least you must try always to give love. At times it may be hard to do so, but in the struggle to see God in all, to be kind and loving toward all, the soul finds freedom. As that freedom begins to manifest, you realize that you are one with Spirit, no longer bound by strong chains of attachment to so many pounds of flesh, with choking desires, passions, moods, and emotions. You are not this body. You are the soul, blissful and immortal.

"When this 'I' shall die, then will I know who am I." Our enemy is that "I," the ego. How to overcome it? By right action, service, striving always to adhere to truth rather than what we want to believe, by meditation, and by practicing the presence of God as continuously as we can during activity.

* Matthew 22:37.
† Matthew 22:39.

Learn to Reside in the Inner Realm

Strive to remain more interiorized. Don't live too much on the surface of life. By this I mean don't allow yourself to be too sensitive, constantly stirred up by the emotions and the demands of the body and by external conditions. Try to remain in the inner stillness of the soul. That is where your real home is, not in this world, not in the temporal security of human relationships and material possessions. That inner realm is where heaven is.

Do the best you can to be more cognizant of that inner world, where you can walk with God and talk with God, and hear His silent assurance that you are His own. This blissful relationship with God cannot come in any other way than by learning to reside more within, in the "interior castle" of which St. Teresa spoke. When your yearning for God is sincere and wholehearted, the moment you go within and silently utter the name of the Divine Beloved, your heart overflows with joy and love. This is what all of us want. No words can describe this joy, this overwhelming love. I understand how easy it is for saints to spend a whole lifetime observing a vow of silence, because there is so much blissful conversation within between God and His true devotees. Saints prefer not to speak much, lest the exploding bombshells of their words drown out the sweet voice of God within.

May Divine Mother bless each one of you, awakening within you a deeper understanding, a steadfast longing, a fervent devotion. March steadily, faithfully, devotedly along the path until you reach the Ultimate Goal.

You have nothing to fear, nothing to worry about when you live your life for God. You have only to follow this simple prescription: keep steady faith in God and Guru to the end of life; meditate deeply and do your Kriya* faithfully; pray for deeper devotion. ❏

---

* Reference to Kriya Yoga, the scientific yoga meditation technique that is the foundation of the path of Self-Realization Fellowship.

SRF Calendars

2019 Inner Reflections
Engagement Calendar

Visit our Inner Reflections gallery at:
www.ircalendar.org

Breathtaking imagery from the world's top nature
photographers and inspirational quotations by
Paramahansa Yogananda

128 pages, 53 color photos
Double wire-O binding
Available in:

- English
- German
- Italian
- Spanish

$13.95

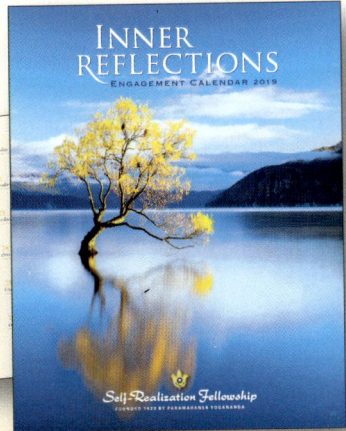

2019 Wall Calendar

Featuring 12 stunning photographs that depict locations of
spiritual sanctuary and beauty closely associated with the life
and work of Paramahansa Yogananda

Printed on high quality glossy stock, 12½" x 9½"
$14.00

www.srfbooks.org

Light for Our Difficult Times

Sri Mrinalini Mata served as SRF/YSS president from 2011 to 2017. The following is an inspirational letter she sent to devotees worldwide for September – October 2016.

Dear One,

Daily events often remind us of the turmoil the world is going through as it strives to cast off the spiritual and material ignorance of past ages. But Gurudeva Paramahansa Yogananda assured us that we are in an era of upward evolution, and held before us a vision of ultimate hope and optimism amid the temporary ups and downs. You can infuse your own life with that positive spirit by refusing to become apprehensive or discouraged — by daily tapping into the freedom and divine strength with which God has endowed all souls.

We are made in His image, and within us is the capacity to anchor ourselves in a reality higher than the troubling drama of duality — to be free as God is free; to unite with His transcendent consciousness, love, and joy. To discover that truth is the purpose of our lives and the ultimate solution to the suffering and inharmony in this world.

Maya tries to keep us bound to the material world, making us feel small and vulnerable to outer circumstances. It causes the ego to become oversensitively reactive with fear, worry, or other negative emotions that weaken the will and narrow one's vision. But Gurudeva urges us not to accept that illusion of helplessness; to affirm instead that our minds and wills are portals to God's omniscient mind and His almighty will. If we keep those inner portals open by using the mind and will rightly, even challenging outer conditions become opportunities to bring out our soul's innate courage and capabilities. Thus we become a positive influence on our daily environment rather than helplessly reacting to it.

"The world will change as the hearts of individuals change," Guruji told us. That change begins with control of our own consciousness. Meditate daily; and daily absorb some of the encouraging, revitalizing truths in Gurudeva's teachings. You will thereby strengthen your faith in God and in yourself, and reinforce your incentive to attune your life with His eternal laws. When you choose to give the Divine Harmony first place in your heart — to live a life of integrity, and to treat others with kindness, understanding, and thoughtfulness — know that you are removing a major cause of suffering and discord in this world: selfishness, and the isolation and strife it fosters.

To live in this world as divine beings, we need to expand our consciousness beyond the little self. What greater answer to the world's troubles could there be than the ancient science of Kriya Yoga, gifted to us by our far-seeing Gurus as the salvation-bringing solution to what they knew we would confront in this modern age? It gives us the means to reverse the outward-flowing life energy that ties us to this chaotic world and to take our awareness within — into the sacred silence of the soul beyond the reach of duality. There we experience the healing touch of God's fathomless peace and His infinite transforming love, which overflows the heart and silently embraces everyone we meet. Guru's blessings and my own constant heartfelt prayers reach out to you as you travel that inner path to freedom from *maya*-dreams and fears, enlarging the circle of your love to radiate to all — as part of your greater Self — God's unifying, peace-giving presence.

God and Gurudeva bless you always,

Sri Mrinalini Mata

Letter from Dr. Karan Singh

Mrinalini Mata received this letter from Dr. Karan Singh, who is a member of India's Upper House of Parliament, the Rajya Sabha, and a former ambassador to the United States. He is also the author of several books of poetry and essays on philosophy and political science. A few of his essays have appeared in Self-Realization *magazine.*

4th November 2016

Dear Mrinalini Mataji,

I have read with pleasure your circular letter for September–October. We are indeed going through a very troubled period in human history. On one hand, science and technology have achieved amazing results which could benefit humanity; on the other, the forces of fanaticism and violence have also raised their head and are creating havoc around the world.

I agree that in the midst of the present turmoil, we all need to deepen our inner perception and move towards spiritual growth.

With kind regards,

Yours sincerely,

Karan Singh

Tuning In to God's Omnipresence:

A Mother's Message of Divine Love

A talk by Sri Mrinalini Mata

"HOW – TO – LIVE" AUDIO SERIES
The Teachings of Paramahansa Yogananda

AN INFORMAL TALK BY
SRI MRINALINI MATA
President and Spiritual Head (2011–2017) of
Self-Realization Fellowship/Yogoda Satsanga Society of India

Tuning In to God's Omnipresence

A Mother's Message of Divine Love

Self-Realization Fellowship

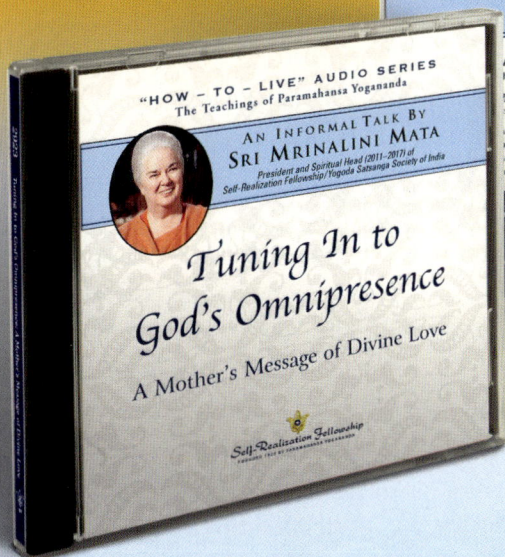

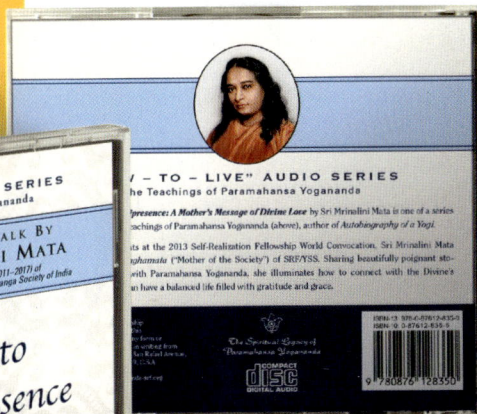

In this talk to participants at the 2013 Self-Realization Fellowship World Convocation, Sri Mrinalini Mata expresses her love as *sanghamata* ("Mother of the Society") of SRF/YSS. Sharing beautifully poignant stories of her experiences with Paramahansa Yogananda, she illuminates how to connect with the Divine's omnipresence—so one can have a balanced life filled with gratitude and grace.

www.srfbooks.org

In Memoriam:
Sister Subrata
1921 – 2018

Sister Subrata, a much-loved nun and ordained minister of Self-Realization Fellowship, peacefully passed away on April 23, 2018. A beloved friend and counselor to many monastics and lay disciples, her lifelong dedication to Paramahansa Yogananda's teachings inspired countless people.

Born Eva Ingeborg Richter in Dresden, Germany, on March 29, 1921, Sister Subrata lived in London and Egypt as a young woman before moving to South America to teach schoolchildren. It was during her time there that she read *Autobiography of a Yogi*. In 1960, she made her first visit to SRF's International Headquarters in Los Angeles, where she met Sri Daya Mata and enrolled for the *Self-Realization Fellowship Lessons*. In 1961, she entered the SRF monastic order.

During her nearly sixty years as a renunciant in the ashrams of Paramahansa Yogananda, Sister Subrata served the SRF work in various ways, including assisting with the translation of Paramahansaji's teachings, supervising the mailing of the *SRF Lessons,* and helping to counsel and guide young nuns of the order.

After residing at the SRF International Headquarters for almost twenty-five years, Sister Subrata was transferred to Front Royal, Virginia, to serve as administrator and minister-in-charge at the newly established SRF Greenfield Ashram and Retreat. In addition to nurturing the growth of this SRF location, she traveled to various cities in the eastern U.S., Europe, and Latin America to conduct inspirational programs on Paramahansaji's teachings. She also presided at dedication ceremonies for SRF centers in Washington, D.C.; New York City; Atlanta, Georgia; and Itter, Austria.

Sister Subrata was a leader of SRF's annual summer program for girls for nearly two decades, especially helping to lay a solid foundation during its formative years. A nun who served with Sister at the time commented on how she interacted with the girls: "She had a way of reaching them and turning them to Master and making them feel very supported. It was an inspiration to see how she worked with the girls and also reached out to the staff." Sister Subrata often led the girls in *kirtan* chanting, and many were moved by the love and devotion that poured forth from her upon these occasions.

In a message that was read at her memorial service at the Mother Center, Brother Chidananda commended highly Sister Subrata's life of complete dedication and concluded with the following words:

"Every soul who lives wholeheartedly for God — for communion with Him and loving service to his children — leaves footprints for others to follow. As we send to our dear Sister Subrata our divine love and friendship, and our appreciation for everything she did for Master's work and his devotees, may we draw inspiration from her selfless life to play our own roles ever centered in God and Guru, allowing Their love and wisdom to flow through all we do." ❑

Becoming Humble Bearers of Light

By Brother Ishtananda

Excerpts from the enclosed recording...

This evening I would like to talk about humility in a very specific way: in terms of being "humble light-bearers," as opposed to "egotistical doom-and-gloomers." I know this phrase might sound kind of funny, but there are spiritual principles here that are worth discussing.

Think about how God creates: In the beginning were thoughts of God, and then the beautiful, luminous astral energy; and finally that energy became compacted into this gross material plane. We are God's children, and we create in exactly the same way. Depending on the power of our thoughts

and the amount of energy we put into them, they manifest on this physical plane. It is like we own a broadcasting station: What kind of programs are we broadcasting? Are they about love, beauty, truth, light, joy? Or are they about disease, death, and destruction?

Master wrote: "The fruits of one's spiritual awakening are a blessing not only on one's own life, but the world at large.... The actions of each individual leave electromagnetic etchings in his brain, influencing his future actions; and they also leave vibrational traces in the ether, which register in and influence the minds of others."

When we talk about "dark and light," it is not just poetic. There is the darkening power of *maya,* or Satan, which obscures the light of God and the divine qualities inherent in that light. But when we think positive, uplifting thoughts — when we create beauty and harmony, when we express love, kindness, compassion — that veil of *maya* becomes more sheer, letting more of God's light out into the world. But when we concentrate on the opposite, it makes the veil more and more opaque.

The greatest way of bringing in more light is through communion with God in meditation. Each and every one of us can *know* we are children of that Higher Power. Experiencing this, we naturally become humble light-bearers, realizing it is God's light reflecting through us. Master spoke of "thousands of Kriya Yogis scattered like shining jewels over the earth." Through deep meditation, let us become those shining jewels, reflecting the light of that Higher Power.

LISTEN TO THE ENCLOSED CD FOR THE REST OF BROTHER ISHTANANDA'S TALK.

SRF minister Brother Ishtananda, an SRF monk for more than forty years, is currently in charge of the Self-Realization Fellowship Hidden Valley Ashram in Escondido, California. Prior to that he was a minister at SRF's Hollywood Temple for many years. This issue's CD features a talk he gave at the SRF World Convocation in Los Angeles in 2009.

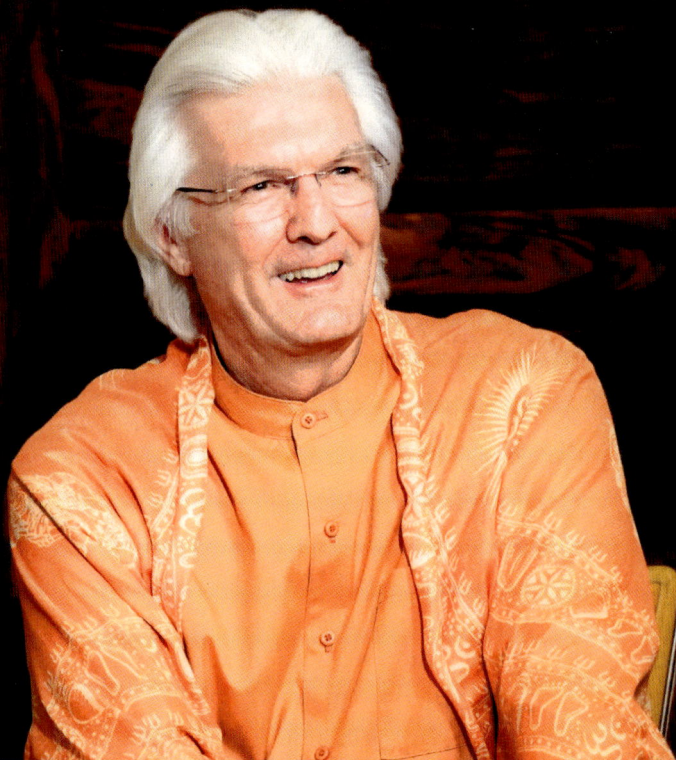

Spiritual Study

A Door to the Guru's Loving Presence

By Brother Chidananda

Based on a satsanga *given by Brother Chidananda on May 18, 2003, to postulant monks in training at the SRF Encinitas Ashram Center*

Excellent questions have been submitted on the subject of studying Paramahansa Yogananda's teachings. In fact, it was a moving experience reading them over, because it took me back to some of the experiences and some of the thoughts and feelings that I had as a young devotee just beginning the monastic path.

The first two questions are linked, in a way. The first one is: "Master* has written many books and it seems impossible to study them all — even in a whole lifetime! What is the way to study that will give the most benefits?" And then the second question: "You are marooned on a desert island and have only one book of Master's. Which book would you take and why?"

Let me start with answering the second question: I would take *all* of them. You are probably thinking: "Wait a minute, that's not the rule, you can only take one of them." But I say that in taking one of them, if you know how to study the Guru's teachings, you *are* taking all of them. The reason for that — and this really gets down to the basic purpose of study as a spiritual technique — is that each work of Master's is a door to Master himself, a door into his presence.

PURPOSE OF SPIRITUAL STUDY IS ATTUNEMENT

Probably the most important point that Guruji made with respect to spiritual study was when he said: "When I am gone, the teachings will be the guru. Through the teachings you will be in tune with me and the great Gurus who sent me." That, in a nutshell, describes the purpose of spiritual study. It is really not about intellectual knowledge or education in the sense of getting an advanced degree in theology. Rather, it is about attunement with the guru. As it is said in India, a true guru is

---

* Disciples of Paramahansa Yogananda often refer to him by the title *Guru,* or its closest English equivalent, *Master.* A true God-illumined *guru* is one who, in his attainment of self-mastery, has realized his identity with the omnipresent Spirit and so is uniquely qualified to lead others to God-union.

a living scripture. That is why I say, if you take any one work of Master's — be it *Autobiography of a Yogi,* the *SRF Lessons, Whispers from Eternity,* one of the books of his lectures* — and truly understand the principle of using study as a means to put yourself in the Guru's presence and attune yourself to him, then you are tapping into the whole ocean of his wisdom.

As the first question rightly pointed out, Master's teachings are indeed vast. And yet by tuning in with Master himself, you are tuning in with the entirety of his works. Gradually experiencing the power of the connection with the Guru that comes through the devotional study of his teachings has been one of the most exciting and sustaining things in my spiritual life over the years.

Using Study to Develop Devotion

The next question goes a little bit deeper into this same subject: "From your experience, does study help in the development of the intellect alone or does it also contribute to development of devotion, attunement to God and Gurus, and one's own Self-realization?"

Yes to all of them. Concentrated study does develop intellectual understanding of the teachings and their philosophy. However, we all know that we did not come here to be ministers of intellect, "walking encyclopedias" who can just quote line and verse from all of Master's books. That is not it at all. Our goal is to be in the Guru's divine presence. And as our spiritual lives unfold over the years, spiritual study helps us to continuously feel Master's guidance by being in contact with his intuitive, inward, silent voice.

One of the disciples who really understood Guruji's teachings, and who is such an example for us, was Sri Gyanamata.†

---

* Paramahansa Yogananda's *Collected Talks and Essays* series (published by Self-Realization Fellowship).

† In giving her the monastic name of Gyanamata ("Mother of Wisdom"), Paramahansaji explained that for her it signified "Mother of Wisdom Through Devotion."

Knowing that she was very well-educated on many subjects, and especially on the subject of India's philosophy and saints, Master once told her that he wondered how it was that she could be so intellectual and at the same time so devotional. In response, she wrote a note to him (which appears in her book, *God Alone*) that in part said: "I knew that I had never read for the purpose of study and scholarship....I read because I wanted to be in the company of the saints."

"[Study] is really not about intellectual knowledge or education in the sense of getting an advanced degree in theology. Rather, it is about attunement with the guru."

And out of that deep study emerged a person who had such wisdom, and yet such devotion, that even when she would walk into a room where Master was, she never asked him any questions. She would simply *pranam*, take the dust of his feet, and then humbly and quietly leave. Why? Because she had everything she needed in that interior communion with him. For us "to be in the company of the saints" means to be in the company of our Guru. And by being in his company we develop that devotion that brings the greatest wisdom.

SPIRITUAL STUDY IS AN INTEGRAL FACET OF A TRULY BALANCED LIFE

Spiritual study is part of the spiritually balanced life that our Guru recommended for monastics and householders alike. This balanced life includes meditation, service, study of his teachings and introspection, physical exercise, wholesome fun and recreation, and times of silence and solitude. These aspects are important for anyone wanting to follow the *sadhana** taught by Paramahansa Yogananda. The wonderful thing about the life that Guruji has outlined for us is that it does

---

* I.e., path of spiritual discipline.

not depend on any one of these things alone. Each balances out and assists the others.

For instance, you will find that if you are going through a dry period in meditation, then by throwing yourself with enthusiasm and devotion into service, you are still able to maintain your connection with Master. Study is *very* powerful when we may not be feeling that we are making progress in meditation or our work assignments, when perhaps these activities feel like a chore. If we have the right attitude toward study, then we are still putting ourselves into Guruji's presence every day. Meditation, service, study — all these things are for one goal, and that is to keep us in tune with the Guru, and ultimately to become one with his God-united consciousness.

BECOMING RECEPTIVE THROUGH STUDY TO WHO YOU REALLY ARE

This next question goes right to the heart of study as a spiritual technique: "Will you speak about *svadhyaya*? Does it have a practical application? What is its essence? How does it relate to Self-realization?"

Svadhyaya is an ancient Sanskrit word, and it is one of the *niyamas* of Patanjali* that has to do with spiritual study. Sanskrit is a language from a higher age, and there is so much more to any of these concepts than what might first appear on the surface when they are translated into English.

One time, when Guruji was working at his desert retreat, dictating his translation of and commentary on the Bhagavad Gita, he gave a translation of a particular Sanskrit passage. One of his secretaries said, "Master, you translated that phrase as

---

* *Niyamas* are five prescriptive principles of conduct enjoined on yogis seeking Self-realization. They consist of purity of body and mind (*shaucha*), contentment in all circumstances (*santosha*); self-discipline (*tapas*); introspective study of the scriptures (*svadhyaya*); and devotion to God and Guru (*ishvara-pranidhana*). In the Eightfold Path of Yoga set forth by the ancient sage Patanjali, *niyamas* constitute the second step.

meaning such and so, but this other edition that I have says that it means *this* — why did this other translator write that?" And Master just chuckled and expressed amusement at the attempts of intellectual scholars to grasp the Gita's deep truths without having God-realization. During this period he was in an extremely high state of divine consciousness, and hour after hour he was bringing out the truths in that scripture, speaking from direct perception. Mrinalini Mata (who was present) has told us that once, after commenting on or translating a particular Sanskrit phrase, he exclaimed in delight, just like a little child: "I got it! I got it! God showed it to me!" In other words, God had given him the true meaning of that Sanskrit verse, which in some cases had never before been fully elucidated. There was no ego-attachment to what he was expressing — it was never an attitude of "See how great I am, that I can perceive these things." He was just completely caught up in the thrill of what God was revealing to him. That is what makes Master's teachings unbelievably great: they are a direct revelation. And as he said in his introduction to the book, there are truths in his Gita commentary that had never been expressed in English before.

So, *svadhyaya,* as part of the *yamas* and *niyamas* of Yoga, in some ways means "self-study," "contemplation"; but in the context of spiritual study, let's consider another aspect of what this concept means. Our Guru went right to the essence of it when he said that one of the implications of this spiritual prescription, one of the ways you can express it in English, is "the repetition of scripture to oneself." If we think about applying this as a practical method, then it relates to what we are trying to do when we are studying — allowing the concepts

"What we are trying to do when we are studying [is] allowing the concepts expressed in Master's words to sink deeply into ourselves by repeated, concentrated reading and assimilation."

expressed in Master's words to sink deeply into ourselves by repeated, concentrated reading and assimilation. As we make our consciousness receptive through this process, those divine perceptions become the defining thoughts or trends of our own consciousness. I remember something Brother Premamoy* once said about study when I was a postulant: "Each day's study period provides the bricks that are going to build the house of your own Self-realization." Then he chuckled and said, "What do you think you are going to use to build that house — all the junk that you absorbed from the world before you came onto this path?" This is so true. We come with such baggage — not only from the way the world is today, but also from our own habits and *samskaras,* our mental tendencies from this life and from the past. All these are manifesting in our attitudes and in the habitual way that we react to things, as well as in our general outlook on life. All these influences that we have internalized result in the mental makeup — the "second nature" or ego personality — that covers our pure soul nature. And it really runs us like a programmed robot until we have progressed spiritually to a greater degree.

The Guru, with the liberating thoughts and perceptions that flow from his divinely attuned consciousness, is gradually replacing all that old baggage of ours with the right attitudes, concepts, and wisdom that enable us to understand our innate divinity: "This is what I really am — not what the world tries to impose on me, not what *maya* tries to impose on me, but what I see in the mirror of my Guru and in my Guru's teachings." At some point, we glimpsed in the mirror of our Guru — in his love, his joy, his divine consciousness — the truth: "That is what I can become!" And this revelation was so inspiring that it motivated all of us here to completely dedicate ourselves to following this blessed path. That is what studying

---

* Brother Premamoy (1910–1990) was responsible for the spiritual training of the postulant monks for more than twenty-five years.

Master's teachings will continue to give to us — the inspiration to realize who we really are.

TAKING THE VIBRATION OF THE GURU'S WORDS INTO YOUR MEDITATIONS

The next question is: "Master wrote in the poem 'When I Am Only a Dream':* 'When you can no longer talk with me, read my *Whispers from Eternity*. Eternally through it I will talk with you.' Does Master mean literally that only *Whispers* has that special blessing or is there a broader interpretation? In other words, 'Read my writings — *Lessons,* books, or anything I have written — to receive that blessing.'"

Yes, he meant it literally. And yes, it also has a wider application to our Guru's other writings. The point is, when Master wrote that poem in 1940 very few of his books were available. *Autobiography of a Yogi* was not published yet. Aside from the *Lessons,* there was only *Whispers* and a few other, smaller books such as *Scientific Healing Affirmations.* So, in one sense, yes, he definitely meant it literally for *Whispers.*

Using *Whispers from Eternity* as a means of attunement with the Guru is something that I have really grown into over the years. When I first came on the path, the devotional style and the approach of this book did not resonate with me right away. But as time went on and I took those Whispers into my meditations, my perspective changed. Now I see that they are such beautiful windows into spiritual perceptions that Master had. And it is not just that *he* had them — he is also saying, "You can have this, too."

Taking one of those Whispers and working with it very much helped me learn how to meditate for longer periods of time. Try that — take those prayer-poems into your meditations and work with them, affirming them deeply, particularly

---

* From *Songs of the Soul* by Paramahansa Yogananda (published by Self-Realization Fellowship).

in a longer meditation each week. It does not take much effort to memorize them — pick one that sparks in you: "I'd love to experience this. This resonates with me." In meditation really dwell on the imagery and the perception that Master is giving; and as you get into it over the course of twenty minutes, thirty minutes, or longer, you will begin to see the depths of blessing that Master can channel through the effort that you are making. His perception flows into your perception.

That is what he is talking about when he says, "Eternally through it I will talk with you." What does "talk with you" actually mean? The Guru is not going to become like someone speaking through a radio earpiece, telling you: "Now do this, turn left, turn right, watch out — there's a hole in the ground up there." No. Master again and again spoke about how, when God and Guru talk with you, it is through divine vibration — the *Aum* vibration, that feeling of Their presence. Through that vibratory presence Master is guiding and encouraging you and, most of all, making you feel how close he is and how he cares for you — how he is right there with you at all times.

RIGHT ATTITUDE TOWARD THE HIGH STANDARD IN THE TEACHINGS

Probably one of the things that inspired us to come onto this path is that our Guru held before us a vision of divine perfection. That is a high standard — and by no means a casual undertaking nor something that is always going to be fun or easy. Sometimes this leads devotees to question: "How can I possibly measure up? Maybe I'm not really good enough. Can I really make it?"

I believe that the next question that was submitted comes from that concern:

"I'm sure that all judgment emanates from my own consciousness. Nevertheless, do you think that the language in the teachings may someday be updated so as not to foster these judgmental reactions? It is difficult for one like myself with low self-esteem (a destructive form of ego-consciousness) to read the *Lessons* without getting down on myself. I've read other, more recent spiritual literature which does not trigger this response but conveys the same principles. Could you comment on this?"

First of all, I think the most interesting thing here is the way in which the question is written: It really answered itself in the very first line, where the person said, "I'm sure that all judgment emanates from my own consciousness." That is the truth. The guru is a flawless mirror; and what he is holding up is, on the one hand, an image of what we can be — actually of what we really are: a perfect soul. Yet at the same time, that mirror works so that whatever we project into it comes right

back at us. So this is a good insight — judgment comes from our own consciousness.

If we think that our Guru is going to reprimand us if we are not already perfect, this is a total projection and a perfect example of that "junk" that we brought with us — the baggage that we mentioned earlier. Far from fostering negativity about ourselves, Master's teachings are helping to replace it, to dredge out that unhealthy attitude.

So, moving to the next part of the question, about updating the teachings to lessen the negative self-judgments this devotee is experiencing, I would say this: When we see that all judgment comes from one's own consciousness, then why would we want the teachings to be changed because of something in our own attitude? Now, I understand where this question is coming from; and to answer it we really ought to have a whole separate class on "how to use the SRF teachings to foster a healthy sense of self-esteem." There is nothing more powerful than what Master teaches for giving us a *real* sense of self-esteem — based on knowing one's true Self, the soul.

But to speak of "updating the teachings" would imply that because Guruji wrote these things fifty, sixty, seventy, eighty years ago that they are now getting to be a little bit passé and beginning to show their age. But I tell you, the more you get into our Guru's teachings, the more you see that the *opposite* is true. What he said will not even be fully understood by the world at large for another 100 or 200 years, as the overall consciousness of humanity evolves into a higher age. But let us speak specifically to the point of how to read the sometimes-challenging spiritual prescriptions in the *Lessons* without getting down on oneself. Someone else recently mentioned to me something similar, saying, "In the *Lessons* and in Master's other writings so many of the passages have statements that include, 'You must do this,' or 'You should do this.'" This person was hearing a constant repetition of "you should" or "you must."

For some people that very easily translates into: "If you are not doing these things then you are no good." So how can we remove that self-created interpretive overlay from what Master is telling us and get the fullest benefit and blessing of studying his teachings?

*"There is nothing more powerful than what Master teaches for giving us a **real** sense of self-esteem — based on knowing one's true Self, the soul."*

Here is how I look at it: Let us think back and trace the chain of events that led us to this present moment. Keep in perspective that lifetimes have been spent in trying this and that to get happiness and fulfillment, and running into one kind of frustration, one kind of disaster, after another. Gradually, after who knows how long, we began to think, "There's got to be more to life than just the superficial." Then we started looking for spiritual teachings in books, in listening to one teacher or another. Through this searching we got a glimpse of the possibilities of life and what life is all about. But still that core of frustration and anguish was not assuaged in our hearts and souls. Wordlessly, or maybe with words, our whole being eventually became a prayer to God, saying: "Free me. Take care of me. Show me the way out of this." And that is when the greatest blessing came — God responded by sending the Guru and the Guru's teachings. At that point we said to Master, "I want what you have. Show me the way." As Arjuna says in the Gita, "Teach me, whose refuge is in Thee."* That is the call of the soul to the Guru.

So when you are studying the *Lessons,* you have to remember that when Guruji says, "You must do this" and "You should do that," he is not scolding or lecturing you! He is simply answering the question that we all asked: "Master, how can I find

---

* *God Talks With Arjuna: The Bhagavad Gita* II:7.

God?" When you are studying his teachings, if you have the tendency to feel any kind of a negative reaction, just remember that when you encounter a passage that says, "You should do that," you have to preface it with words that are not there but that are implied. Preface it with, "*If you want to find God, you should do this, this, this, and this; and you should not do this, this, and this.*" This gives it a whole different vibration. Remember that you asked: "How can I be free? How can I find God?" The Guru is really just answering the deepest soul call from within us. He is saying: "There is no reason to feel bad when I say these things to you. After all, you are the one that asked me to tell you!" Try this line of thinking if you find yourself in this position.

Remember: Our Guru has given a voluminous teaching, and he doesn't expect us to master everything all at once! He even said, "If you practice one millionth of the things that I tell you, you will reach God." If we are making a sincere effort to progress — especially with the undaunted attitude of "I will never give up!" — we can be sure that he is pleased with us.

We have really just scratched the surface of this profound subject. But for now, the main thing I want you to remember is to think of spiritual study not as memorizing a lot of philosophical concepts, but instead as *svadhyaya,* self-study in the sense of "repeating of scripture to oneself." This means replacing all of our harmful, negative, limiting ideas and attitudes and mindsets about ourselves with the truth that we are made in God's image. "What Master has, what Master feels, what Master realizes, I can realize. That is what I am." That is what study of his teachings is gradually doing over the years: drop by drop it is replacing those stale, polluted waters of delusion that we are constantly imbibing in this world with the pure crystal spring of our Guru's divine consciousness. In that purified awareness, we become free. ❐

HOW TO ORDER

Our full selection of books, recordings, calendars,
and devotional items can be ordered in a variety of ways:

Online

www.srfbooks.org

By phone

(MasterCard, Visa, or American Express)

(818) 549-5151

Monday–Friday, 9:00 a.m.–12:30 p.m.;
1:30–4:00 p.m. (Pacific time)

By fax

U.S.A./Canada (800) 801-1952

Outside U.S.A./Canada (818) 549-5100

Our fax line is open 24 hours a day, 7 days a week.

Self-Realization Magazine

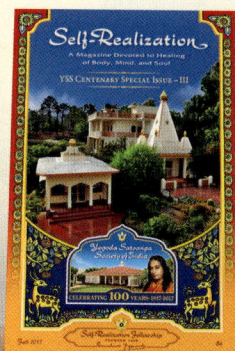

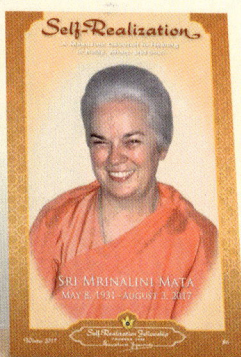

Paramahansa Yogananda created *Self-Realization* magazine in 1925 to bring inspiration and encouragement to those seeking a deeper spiritual truth.

Subscribe today:
www.yogananda-srf.org/srm

ago by neurobiologist Jack Feldman at UCLA, who collaborated on the new research. It has since been found in humans. Unlike the cardiac pacemaker, which is in the heart as you might expect, the breathing pacemaker is in the brain. It consists of about 3,000 neurons in the medulla.

Researchers have been working to identify those neurons and their roles. One of Krasnow's graduate students, Kevin Yackle, now at the University of California, San Francisco, analyzed the neurons genetically and found that the pacemaker's 3,000 brain cells can be grouped into 65 subtypes. In an earlier study, Yackle discovered that one of those subtypes, encompassing some 200 neurons, directly controls sighing in mice. Activate those neurons and the mice start sighing. Inactivate them and the mice never sigh. (In both mice and men, a sigh is a double-sized breath.)

In the new study, Yackle singled out another set of neurons, 175 this time, and inactivated them. Yackle, Krasnow, and their colleagues thought they would find the same sort of effect as with sighing. Instead, nothing happened. "It was actually very disappointing initially because the breathing patterns did not change," says Krasnow. But Yackle kept watching the mice, and he noticed that while their breathing hadn't changed, their behavior had. "The mice had become chill," says Krasnow. "They were laid back."

Usually, when put in a new environment, like the chamber for measuring their breathing, mice explore by sniffing all around. These mice just hung quietly in the corner and groomed themselves, which Krasnow says is "the kind of thing mice do when they're calm and relaxed."

What Yackle eventually determined is that the 175 neurons he had inactivated extend from the pacemaker to the brain's arousal center, the locus coeruleus. That arousal center tells the rest of the brain whether to wake up or chill out, depending on what's going on. Like the dashboard of your car letting you know to get gas or air in your tire, these neurons appear to monitor the other neurons in the breathing pacemaker and then tell the brain whether it needs to respond. Just as you would keep driving until you ran out of fuel without a gas gauge, without that neural signal mice put in a new environment might as well be home in their nests. It's likely that the same setup will be found in humans.

"We now know that the breathing center directly controls the activity of higher order brain functions," says Krasnow. "There's a feedback circuit. Now we can understand better how this control of the breathing center changes the rest of the brain." Beyond helping all of us in our everyday lives, the research could someday lead to therapies for deadly problems like sleep apnea or Sudden Infant Death Syndrome (SIDS).

For those who've long believed in the powerful effects of breathing, this is proof they were right. For those who were skeptical, like Krasnow himself, this is hard evidence that changing your breathing can change your state of mind. If you want to wake yourself up, try speeding up your breathing. And if you need to calm down, you really should take a deep breath. It's just what the neuroscientists ordered. ❐

MP3 Downloads $1.99 EACH ◄

From *Self-Realization* Magazine Audio Talks

Yoga: The Quintessence of Spirituality ▼
A talk by
Brother Chidananda

In His Presence ▼
A talk by
Sri Mrinalini Mata

The Good Fortune of the Disciple ▼
A talk by
Swami Bhavananda

"Banat, Banat, Ban Jai!" ▼
A talk by
Swami Smarananda

Find these inspirational talks, and many more at
www.srfbooks.org

A New Era for SRF Publications

Brother Chidananda Dedicates New Digital Equipment

On July 3, 2018, SRF took another step towards the release of the new expanded and enhanced edition of the *Self-Realization Fellowship Lessons* with the dedication of major new equipment at its Publications Center. SRF President Brother Chidananda presided at this special landmark event.

For decades SRF used older technology — an offset production process that was powered by a large two-color press donated in 1991. In selecting the new equipment, SRF opted to switch to a digital production process that utilizes the latest technology. The main pieces include a digital color printing press; a black-and-white printer for books; an automated assembly line that cuts, folds, collates, and assembles the printed sheets into various publications; a book binder for creating paperback books; and an automated envelope inserter for the *Lessons* and other mailings.

(Above) Brother Chidananda cuts ceremonial ribbon in front of the new digital color press. *(Below)* He then inaugurates the press by using a computer workstation to initiate the first printing job.

A MESSAGE OF HEARTFELT GRATITUDE

Joining Brother Chidananda at the July 3 dedicatory event were members of the Self-Realization Fellowship/Yogoda Satsanga Society of India Boards of Directors, other senior SRF monastics, and dozens of the monks, lay members, and employees who serve at the SRF Publications Center.

Standing near where former SRF president Sri Daya Mata stood when she dedicated the SRF Publications Center at a similar event in 1991 (*see photos below*), Brother Chidananda welcomed the assemblage. Following are excerpts from his remarks:

I can't tell you with what joy and gratitude I am here today at our SRF Publications Center. Think for a moment about the significance of this building where the printing is done for our Self-Realization Fellowship publications: the books, *Self-Realization* magazine, the *Self-Realization Fellowship Lessons,* the video and audio recordings, and the beautiful photographs of our Gurus. They all come from this holy location, flowing out to the different countries where people revere and look to our Guru for spiritual light, for upliftment, for courage, for strength — reaching not only SRF's members but also the countless thousands of other souls around the world who increasingly are turning to Gurudeva as their guiding light in their path through life....

Please join me now in expressing our profound and boundless gratitude to all those thousands of dear members around the world who have contributed in whatever way they could to make possible the acquisition of this equipment. No doubt all of them are just as excited as we are with the anticipation of soon holding in their hands the new edition of the *SRF Lessons.*

For additional coverage of this event, including an inspiring video, please visit: www.yogananda-srf.org/newprintingequipment. ❐

Letters to SRF

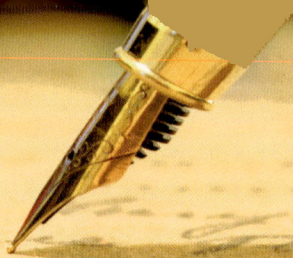

Before I found [Paramahansa Yogananda] my life was a mess and I was living very selfishly. Within six months of having been introduced to him, my whole life was different — no more drinking or smoking, and I was all-around living a better life. Mentally, I am calmer, so much more at peace with daily life and able to deal with trials with calmness and wisdom. Spiritually, I am more aware of God and Guru's constant presence. It is hard to express in words the happiness and eternal gratitude I have found since Guruji came into my life.

— J. C., Florida

This is to thank you from the bottom of our hearts for making it possible for Brother Balananda, Brother Sevananda, and Brahmachari Wolfgang to come to Germany [for a program of classes and meditations in May], to give to so many of us this special present of a very inspiring and spiritually uplifting long weekend. Master's great love, wisdom, and guidance were flowing so freely and strongly through them and their dedication and selfless service were really a wonderful example for all of us!

After a very beautiful Kriya initiation ceremony, the devotees were so happy that they did not want to leave the hall where this sacred event had taken place. The presence and contribution of our dear SRF nuns from the Nuremberg Ashram was so important and much appreciated by all.

As many devotees stated afterwards, we felt it was like a mini-Convocation in Europe and we all left Rosenheim very spiritually enriched and uplifted.

— M. E., Austria

Thank you all so much for my retreat experience [at the SRF Encinitas Retreat], however brief it may have been. I found everything to be extraordinary — the service, the rooms, the temple, the meals, the gardens, the overall atmosphere, the helpfulness of staff, the *everything*. To walk along grounds that

Master himself has walked — and to meditate, looking out at the same horizon, the same view he loved so much. It was most lovely and meaningful. I've visited many sacred and spiritual places in the world but the grounds of the Encinitas Hermitage simply resound with a spiritual sensation I have not quite encountered before. I look forward to a time when I can spend a week here.

— *B. R., Pennsylvania*

I spent five weeks committing the Energization Exercises to memory. They literally changed my life. Prior to learning them I had needed to visit my chiropractor once every five weeks for the prior thirteen years, or my musculature would completely hobble my spine. Since I finished learning these exercises, I have not needed to go back even once. Also, a digestive ailment is in the process of curing.

To me, these are miracles. The Energization Exercises changed my physical life, and my meditations are *way better* as well.

— *J. S., Massachusetts*

The more I meditate, the more I feel that I am not alone — finally! Doubts are gone; I am connected to our Guru; sometimes tears drop down on my face because I feel joy. I have found myself and don't need anymore the approval of somebody else — I finally have *my* approval. The path was very difficult but now I have peace and joy with God.

— *E. V., Brazil*

By profession I am an engineer. I was in a bookshop in Bangalore looking for a book on the Bhagavad Gita. Someone came and gave me *God Talks With Arjuna: The Bhagavad Gita* and said it was very good. I started by reading one verse every day. After a while I started reading my one verse each day plus meditating for five minutes. I started feeling internal joy from these activities. After two years I completed reading the two volumes. During this period my meditation time has increased, to as long as two hours. There is tremendous satisfaction for me after reading the two volumes. All of my doubts are cleared. I know who I am and what I am. Guruji, Paramahansa Yogananda, has taken the task of spreading God's message to all humankind so that each human being will give priority to achieving Self-realization in their life.

— *Anonymous, Oman*

Directory of Temples, Centers, and Meditation Groups

Self-Realization Fellowship/Yogoda Satsanga Society of India

Founded by Paramahansa Yogananda in India in 1917 and in America in 1920 for worldwide dissemination of definite scientific techniques for attaining direct personal experience of God.

Brother Chidananda, President

International Headquarters, Los Angeles, California, U.S.A.

The Mother Center, 3880 San Rafael Avenue (Zip code 90065-3219). Telephone (323) 225-2471. Fax (323) 225-5088. Visiting hours: 9:00 a.m. to 5:00 p.m. Tuesday–Saturday, and 1:00 to 5:00 p.m. Sunday. Closed on Monday. All are welcome.

www.yogananda-srf.org

Self-Realization Fellowship Ashram Centers and Temples

Services are held Thursday at 8:00 p.m. in all temples, except San Diego (7:00 p.m.), Encinitas and Glendale (7:30 p.m.); and Sunday at 11:00 a.m. in all temples except Phoenix (10:00 a.m.). The same lecture is also given at 9:00 a.m. in the Pacific Palisades temple, and at 9:30 a.m. in the Hollywood, Encinitas, and San Diego temples. *(Please refer to the "Schedule of Services," available from the international headquarters or any of the temples listed below, for a complete listing of lectures, meditation services, and other activities.)*

BERKELEY, California: Temple, 3201 Shattuck Avenue (Zip code 94705). Telephone (510) 984-0084.

ENCINITAS, California: Ashram, Retreat, and Hermitage, 215 K St. at Second (Zip code 92024-5040). Telephone (760) 753-2888. Retreat grounds open to the public 9:00 a.m. to 5:00 p.m., Tuesday through Saturday; 11:00 a.m. to 5:00 p.m. Sunday. Closed on Mondays.

Temple: 939 Second Street. Telephone (760) 436-7220 or (760) 753-2888.

Self-Realization Fellowship Retreat, 215 K St., Encinitas, CA (Zip code 92024-5040): guest accommodations and *How-to-Live Retreat* programs. For information call (760) 753-1811 or email encretreat@yogananda-srf.org.

ESCONDIDO, California: SRF Hidden Valley Ashram Center, 16455 Old Guejito Grade Road (Zip code 92027). Tranquil environment where men may stay for brief or extended periods as part of the guest resident "how-to-live" program, participating in the monks' spiritual routine and assisting in the daily activities of the Ashram Center. Please call (760) 749-3399, or email info@hvashram.org, or visit www.hvashram.org for further information.

FRONT ROYAL, Virginia: SRF Greenfield Retreat, 2660 John Marshall Highway (Zip code 22630). Telephone (540) 635-5062. *How-to-Live Retreat* programs.

FULLERTON, California: Temple, 142 East Chapman Avenue (Zip code 92832). Telephone (714) 525-1291.

GLENDALE, California: Temple, 2146 East Chevy Chase Drive (Zip code 91206). Telephone (818) 543-0800.

HOLLYWOOD, California: Ashram, Temple, and India Hall, 4860 West Sunset Boulevard (Zip code 90027). Telephone (323) 661-8006.

NÜRNBERG, Germany: Ashram, Laufamholzstrasse 369, 90482 Nürnberg, Germany. Telephone 011 49 (911) 50 10 87. Open Tuesday through Saturday from 9:00 a.m. to 5:00 p.m. Closed on Mondays and holidays. If you wish to visit on Sunday afternoon, please call in advance. Visitors are welcome.

PACIFIC PALISADES, California: Ashram, Temple, Retreat, Lake Shrine, and Mahatma Gandhi World Peace Memorial, 17190 Sunset Boulevard (Zip code 90272). Telephone (310) 454-4114. Open to the public 9:00 a.m. to 4:30 p.m., Tuesday through Saturday; noon to 4:30 p.m. Sunday. Closed Mondays and holidays. (Occasionally closed on Saturdays.)

SELF-REALIZATION FELLOWSHIP RETREAT, 17190 Sunset Blvd., Pacific Palisades, CA (Zip code 90272): guest accommodations and *How-to-Live Retreat* programs. For information call (310) 459-4740 or email lsretreat@yogananda-srf.org.

PHOENIX, Arizona: Ashram, Temple, 6111 North Central Avenue (Zip code 85012). Telephone (602) 279-6140.

SAN DIEGO, California: Temple, 3072 First Avenue (Zip code 92103). Telephone (619) 295-0170.

Self-Realization Fellowship Centers and Meditation Groups

SRF centers and meditation groups exist throughout the world to provide places for God-seeking souls to come together for group practice of the Self-Realization techniques of meditation and divine communion. For information about locations, services, and visits by SRF monastics, please visit our website and click on the "Centers & Programs" tab. For additional information please contact SRF Center Department, either by email at CenterDepartment@Yogananda-SRF.org, or by telephone at our international headquarters: 323-225-2471.

Areas in which there are centers and groups are as follows:

UNITED STATES:

ALASKA, ARIZONA, ARKANSAS, CALIFORNIA, COLORADO, CONNECTICUT, DELAWARE, DISTRICT OF COLUMBIA, FLORIDA, GEORGIA, HAWAII, IDAHO, ILLINOIS, INDIANA, IOWA, KANSAS, KENTUCKY, LOUISIANA, MAINE, MARYLAND, MASSACHUSETTS, MICHIGAN, MINNESOTA, MISSISSIPPI, MISSOURI, MONTANA, NEBRASKA, NEVADA, NEW HAMPSHIRE, NEW JERSEY, NEW MEXICO, NEW YORK, NORTH CAROLINA, OHIO, OKLAHOMA, OREGON, PENNSYLVANIA, PUERTO RICO, RHODE ISLAND, SOUTH CAROLINA, TENNESSEE, TEXAS, UTAH, VERMONT, VIRGINIA, WASHINGTON, WISCONSIN.

ARGENTINA, AUSTRALIA, AUSTRIA, BARBADOS, BELGIUM, BOLIVIA, BRAZIL, BRUNEI, BULGARIA, CANADA, CHILE, CHINA, COLOMBIA, COSTA RICA, CROATIA, CUBA, DENMARK, DOMINICAN REPUBLIC, ECUADOR, FIJI, FINLAND, FRANCE, GERMANY, GHANA, GREECE, GUATEMALA, HONDURAS, ICELAND, INDONESIA, IRELAND, ITALY, JAPAN, JORDAN, KENYA, LATVIA, MALAYSIA, MAURITIUS, MEXICO, NETHERLANDS, NEW ZEALAND, NORWAY, PARAGUAY, PERU, PHILIPPINES, PORTUGAL, ROMANIA, RUSSIA, SINGAPORE, SLOVENIA, SOUTH AFRICA, SOUTH KOREA, SPAIN, SWEDEN, SWITZERLAND, TAIWAN, THAILAND, TRINIDAD, TURKEY, UNITED ARAB EMIRATES, UNITED KINGDOM, VENEZUELA, ZAMBIA.

Yogoda Satsanga Society of India

For information about Yogoda Satsanga Society ashrams, activities, branch centers, and groups throughout India, visit www.yssofindia.org or write to General Secretary, Yogoda Satsanga Society of India, Yogoda Satsanga Sakha Math, Paramahansa Yogananda Path, Ranchi 834 001, Jharkhand, India.

Headquarters and Ashram Centers

KOLKATA, West Bengal: Registered office (headquarters), Yogoda Satsanga Math, Dakshineswar, Kolkata — 700 076, West Bengal. Telephone 91-33-2564-5931, 91-33-2564-2366, or 91-33-2564-6208.

RANCHI, Jharkhand: Yogoda Satsanga Sakha Math, Paramahansa Yogananda Path, Ranchi — 834 001, Jharkhand. Telephone 91-651-246-0074, 91-651-246-1578, or 91-651-246-0071.

DWARAHAT, Uttarakhand: Yogoda Satsanga Sakha Ashram, Dwarahat — 263 653, District Almora, Uttarakhand. Telephone 91-5966-244271.

NOIDA, Uttar Pradesh: Yogoda Satsanga Sakha Ashram, B-4 Sector 62, Noida — 201307, Uttar Pradesh. Telephone 91-120-240-0670 or 91-120-240-0671.

Schools and Charitable Medical Dispensaries

Paramahansa Yogananda began his Yogoda Satsanga Society work in India with the founding of a Yogoda "How-to-Live" School and Ashram in 1917, offering balanced training in physical, mental, moral, and spiritual ideals for all-round success in life. These principles have expanded into his now worldwide mission and Kriya Yoga teachings. To serve the humanitarian needs of India, Yogoda Satsanga runs in the name and spirit of Paramahansa Yogananda a number of educational institutions and medical dispensaries. These include seventeen educational institutions for boys and girls, and many homeopathic and allopathic medical dispensaries throughout India, a college with degree programs in arts, commerce, and science, boys' school, girls' school, Sevashram medical clinic with allopathic and homeopathic sections, and an eye clinic, all in Ranchi; a college with degree programs in arts, commerce, science, and education in Palpara; high schools and/or primary schools in Bherir Bazar, Chandigarh, Dwarahat, Ghatal, Kulabahal, Iṣmalichak, Lakhanpur, Palpara, and Payarachak; and medical dispensaries all over India.

Index to Volume 89: Winter 2017 – Fall 2018

Authors

Articles

CD Series

Miscellaneous